March 10, 2008

IMAGES OF

Haleakalā

Photography by

Douglas Peebles

Mutual Publishing

ISBN 10: 1-56647-727-1
ISBN 13: 978-1-56647-727-7

Library of Congress Catalog Card Number: 2005922547

First Printing, April 2007
Second October, 2007

Mutual Publishing, LLC
1215 Center Street, Suite 210
Honolulu, Hawai‘i 96816
Ph: 808-732-1709 / Fax: 808-734-4094
e-mail: info@mutualpublishing.com
www.mutualpublishing.com

Printed in China

The grandeur of Haleakalā as seen from above.

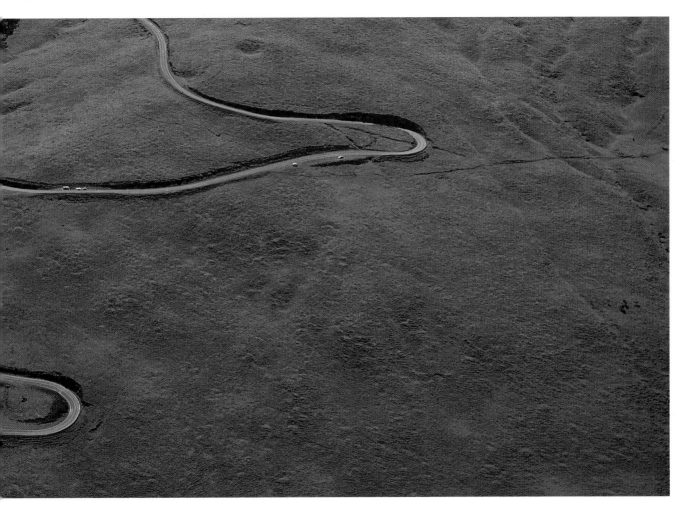

The serpentine highway leading to Haleakalā National Park, the greatest elevation gain in the shortest distance in the world.

The glorious sun rising over Haleakalā, a sight which attracts thousands of early risers each year.

Summit overlooks which reveal moonlike vistas.

Haleakalā, the House of the Sun, so named as Māui the demigod captured the sun here.

Crimson-hued lava adorning the volcanic slopes.

A silver-leafed 'āhinahina, or silversword, gleaming amid a field of lava.

'Āhinahina in full bloom, a floral spectacle that blooms once before dying.

Nēnē, or native Hawaiian geese, which make their home in the Haleakalā wilderness.

A unique sign to protect the endangered nēnē, the state bird of Hawai'i.

Pu'u, or cinder cones (towards the middle of the photo), rising from an ethereal lava landscape.

Hikers enjoying one of several paths within the wilderness area.

A view from Koʻolau Gap overlooking the lush eastern floor of Haleakalā.

Upper Kīpahulu Valley, a vast break in the mountain peak where lava once flowed toward the ocean.

An expansive view of the 10,000-foot peak of Haleakalā, showing the island of Hawai'i in the distance.

Sister volcanoes to Haleakalā, Mauna Kea and Mauna Loa on the island of Hawai'i emerge from the clouds.

Bikers descending the mountain, enjoying a panoramic view of central and west Maui.

Sunrise at Haleakalā in the summertime—an awe-inspiring experience not easily forgotten.

Sugarcane fields of central Maui stretching to the base of Haleakalā.

The western slope of Haleakalā, known locally as Upcountry.

Makawao, known for its rough-and-tumble Hawaiian-style rodeo held on the Fourth of July.

Horses grazing in verdant Upcountry ranchland.

Flowering jacaranda trees which seasonally grace roadsides in Kula.

A protea, one of several exotic flowers grown commercially in Kula flower farms.

A picturesque road indicative of Upcountry's rural lifestyle.

Farmland in Kula, home of the world-famous Maui onion.

A pigtail anthurium growing at Kula Botanical Gardens,
one of several floral showplaces located Upcountry.

Lavender growing at Aliʻi Kula Lavender farm in Kula.

Remote ʻUlupalakua on the southwest slope of Haleakalā.

The northern flank of Haleakalā bordered by the 52-mile road to Hanā,
notable for its 617 curves and 56 bridges.

Koʻolau, one of the forested crevasses carved into the northern slope of Haleakalā.

Wailua, an area known for its spectacular waterfalls.

Four-hundred-foot Waimoku Falls located in the Kīpahulu District of Haleakalā National Park.

Manawainui, a dramatic water-carved gulch on the southern edge of Haleakalā.

Kaupō ranchland, typical of the stark southern lowlands of Haleakalā.

Look for our other titles in the Images series:

O'AHU
IMAGES OF THE GATHERING PLACE
ISBN 1-56647-670-4

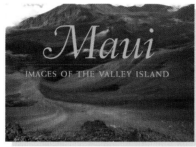

MAUI
IMAGES OF THE VALLEY ISLAND
ISBN 1-56647-602-X

KAUA'I
IMAGES OF THE GARDEN ISLE
ISBN 1-56647-668-2

THE BIG ISLAND
IMAGES OF THE ISLAND OF HAWAI'I
ISBN 1-56647-671-2

VOLCANO
IMAGES OF HAWAI'I'S VOLCANOES
ISBN 1-56647-603-8

HAWAI'I
IMAGES OF THE ISLANDS
ISBN 1-56647-726-3

Visit our website at www.mutualpublishing.com